Dreams: The Money Jars

(What If You Dreamed – About Money?)

New Age/ Dreams with Interpretation

Mary Belle Claude

**Outskirts Press, Inc.
Denver, Colorado**

The opinions expressed in this manuscript are solely the opinions of the author and do not represent the opinions or thoughts of the publisher. The author represents and warrants that s/he either owns or has the legal right to publish all material in this book.

Dreams: The Money Jars (What If You Dreamed - About Money?)
New Age/ Dreams with Interpretation
All Rights Reserved.
Copyright © 2008 Mary Belle Claude
V2.0

Cover Photo © 2008 JupiterImages Corporation. All rights reserved - used with permission.

This book may not be reproduced, transmitted, or stored in whole or in part by any means, including graphic, electronic, or mechanical without the express written consent of the publisher except in the case of brief quotations embodied in critical articles and reviews.

Outskirts Press, Inc.
http://www.outskirtspress.com

ISBN: 978-1-4327-1038-5

Library of Congress Control Number: 2007940241

Outskirts Press and the "OP" logo are trademarks belonging to Outskirts Press, Inc.

PRINTED IN THE UNITED STATES OF AMERICA

My Gift

Everyday as I sit... I'd be thinking about what it is that I have to give to the world... other than my presence of being here. Surely there must be something. I'd look all around my beautiful place ... wondering "what do I have to offer ?" I often looked at my left hand... extended in front of my eyes hoping to see... just pondering what is it?

Maybe... my Dreams ... I mean the ones that come with sleep. I have so many of them and they are interesting ... just maybe other people would want to know of them.

I thinks it's a gift and I could share. It surely is a gift to me. Then also... I could share my own insight and inner knowledge.... as to what my dreams meant for me.

So now, I have three gifts to give in each of my books.

1. The Name Sake dream
2. The Dreams
3. My insights

As I open up and share... I hope they bring you much enjoyment and insights of your own.

A FOUR PART SERIES
    1. DREAMS: A CLEAR PENNY
    2. DREAMS: DOLLARS ON A ROLL
    3. DREAMS: HUNDREDS OF HUNDREDS
    4. DREAMS: MILLIONS CLEARLY STATED

NEW BOOK - " DREAMS: THE MONEY JARS "
   (What if you Dreamed - about Money?)

Foreword ♥

I've had numerous dreams concerning money. They are most enjoyable and make me feel good... but there seems to be an illusiveness about the money.

How I wish with all my heart... I could tell you that... if you dreamed of money... that you would have it. But it just doesn't work that way for me... in real life. Maybe there are those fortunate ones... out there that the money does come to them. For myself... when the money comes at times... its more of a feeling... than seeing it in a dream.

It's a good, good feeling of wealth... and wholeness that money brings to our lives. Dream big! You never know the dreams could just come true!

So... for now... I'll enjoy winning the money and all the other wonderful aspects of prosperity... that my dreams bring to me.

♥

P.S. The dreams contained in this book are a collection of money dreams... that are in my other dream books. Also, included are the name sake dreams for each of the titles of the books. All the dreams are true... with the exception of the name sake dreams.

DREAM REALLY BIG !!!

♥ ♥ ♥

Table of Contents ♥

1. My Gift...i
2. Foreword...iii
3. Table of Contents...v
4. The Dreams
    The Money Jars - Name Sake Dream 1
    A Clear Penny (name sake)...3
    Dollars on a Roll (name sake).......................................5
    Dream Money 7
    Ex-Husband..9
    Gambling at the Pioneer 13
    Get Your Own Towel...15
    Gold Coins 17
    Hundreds of Hundreds (name sake)............................21
    Ice Cream Man...25
    Irish Dream 31
    Leisure Time - Dog in the Box 35
    Millions Clearly Stated (name sake)...........................39
    New Credit Cards...43
    Poker Chips..47
    Roman Coins..49
    The Band..53
    The Big Jackpot 57
    The Casino Hotel Room...59
    The Mafia - Asking Godfather....................................63
    The Violet Ah-Ha Moment..67
    The Wal-Mart Refund..71
    Trees & Money 73

      Who's Driving 77
      Winning..81
5. My Dream Symbols 83
6. The Author 85
7. Last Page..87

The Money Jars ♥
(Name Sake Dream)

    I'm standing at the base of a beautiful mountain. As I look at the scenery... it is so very peaceful... with lush green gardens and clear skies. I don't notice any people or animals around... just the peacefulness. A short distance in front of me ... I see an oriental man. He has his back to me... and he's working on something.
    The scene around him isn't too clear... it's like in a dim light. As I approach him... he turns around. He's middle aged... but looks old with wisdom...like a teacher. He knows what I've come to ask... even before I say it.
    As he moves to one side... I see two beautiful jade stone jars... that are about four feet tall. There is water trickling down the sides of both... as if they are fountains. It seems so fitting as... I can feel the oriental gardens all around me. I look inside the jars...and they are filled with money and gold coins...I'm just looking at them in awe. The man takes a tray... that's just a wooden frame with a screen over it... then he puts handfuls and handfuls of beautiful golden coins on the tray... and then he hands it to me.
    Its like how does he know? I want to have money to complete my project. He says it's for me... to continue on with my work. He also states that... as he removes some of the coins from the jars... they are immediately replaced...as if by the magic of the universe.
    He takes his hands and scoops up more coins... as he starts to put them on the tray... a beautiful orange fancy goldfish falls to the earth. I quickly pick it up... to put it back in the jar of money and water. But instead... the man puts the fish in a clear glass bowl of water on my tray. He now gives me some special food for the goldfish... that's made from grains. I feed some to the fish and put the rest away.

I'm now sitting on a stone bench... looking at the coins and watching the gold fish. I feel so wonderful and prosperous. The man tells me... there is more than enough money for all that I want... to come anytime. The money jars always refill themselves.

This is a very inspirational dream... to know that the universe supplies unlimited amounts of money. Just take what you need and the supply replenishes itself.

The fancy goldfish is symbolic of the truths of prosperity. The man letting me keep the goldfish... means keeping my own truths or ideas of money near me... and to feed these ideas. The man letting me keep the goldfish... means keeping my own truths or ideas of money near me... and to feed those ideas... that he will help in my journey.

A Clear Penny ♥
(The Name Sake Dream)

There I am... a middle age Chinese man... with medium blue work clothes on... walking along a path in China. I can see the hillside with trees and villages in the distance ... but it seems cloudy or maybe gloomy. I feel the heaviness of my life... and striving for better days.

As I'm walking along... I look down at the wet earth by the path... and I see a penny. It has the '1 cent' on the side face up. I bend down to pick it up. Then as I hold the penny in my hands... it starts to grow. It becomes as large as a dinner plate. I'm just standing holding it in awe. Then the penny turns to a clear crystal ... but I can still see the '1 cent' on it.

I look thru the crystal penny at myself... and I now see I'm dressed in a fine silk kimono. I look so healthy and vibrant. The clouds start to disappear... and the sun is shining over a lush beautiful green hillside now. I feel in wonderment of it all. It's all so clear now. How things really are. I see the richness and beauty of life. I am so thankful that... I am truly rich and wealthy.

Some of the near by farmers and some children come closer to me as they could see something has changed. I looked thru my big clear penny and I see each of them rich, well and very happy too.

As I see myself being a man from China... means I'm seeing the male or positive side of myself. The country of China means... an older way of life. The blue work clothes meant... I was working on my spiritual path. I had felt the heaviness of always struggling in life and wanting more, especially ... money ... to create a better life for myself. The penny represented richness in a common sense or cents / sort of speak. As I used my common sense... it grew and turned to crystal. When I viewed myself and my world thru it as ...A Clear Penny ... everything else became clear and rich.

I had received wealth... by looking at things in a brighter light or a new way of understanding. The kimono as clothing represented... a new understanding. Not only that...but my whole world and everyone in it became richer. Looking thru the crystal penny also meant... looking thru to my higher-self for a higher way to reach my goal ... of a better life.

Dollars on a Roll ♥
(The Name Sake Dream)

I'm standing in a very green, dense, lush jungle... and I can hardly see the clear blue humid sky. There are so many plants, tree and vines... I'm really wondering how I'm surviving here. Next, I see some small spots of clear water... and I know there's more water... beneath the leaves and bushes.

I'm trying to find my way... looking for a path. I seem to be alone... just me and this huge overgrown tropical jungle. I feel hot and sticky... and I can feel mosquitoes buzzing close. I'm looking towards some taller trees and... I see what looks like a roll of paper towels on a holder attached to the tree. " Well, that's for me!"

As I get closer... they are green in color... I can hardly wait to wipe the sweat from my face. I grab for them... and as I pull them out and down... I see its really dollar bills. WOW! I use my arm to brush the sweat out of my eyes...and its still dollar bills on a roll. I take them down to take with me.

I start to walk ...and over to the side of me is... a shiny tin storage building... in this jungle? I open the doors to it and... there must be thousands of the rolls of dollar bills.

The dream jumps... then I notice next to me... there is a game show host... with his microphone that has a very long cord. He's saying, "Congratulations! You are the big winner! All this is yours!"

I can hear an audience applauding... but I can't see them. I'm standing still partly in the jungle...and partly on a game show stage. Next, he announces that in addition to the money... " You have won a beautiful home in the location of your choice."

Mary Belle Claude

Then the scene changes some. I see flat golden flagstones on the ground… with water running between them. Then, I hear the game show host say again " It's your choice " referring to the home. He goes on to name several other things I won… a vacation home, a car, etc. Most everything you could dream of… I had won them.

The overgrown jungle represents paths and growth… we take in life… but there seemed too many to follow… or choose between. The water pools in the jungle represented enlightenment…but you couldn't see them in their entirety. By choosing the relief of the paper towels… I hit the biggest prize of all. My path was cleared for me…I was wealthy and the choice was mine… which is truly what I want in life.

Dream Money ♥

I'm sitting with my friend... inside a crowded dark room. There are lots of people around me... and they are talking with each other. It seems to feel okay to be here. I'm telling my friend... I just won the lottery! I feel so excited. I can see the ticket in front of me. He seems quietly excited and very happy for me.

Then I realize... the people there have been waiting... for the out come of the lottery. I don't announce I've won... but they seem to know it... and are celebrating for me. My friend quietly leans over to me... and says, " What are you going to do... with your one hundred million dollars?"

Wow! $100,000,000.00 I was still in shock from actually winning the money... and I could feel so much excitement... it was hard to talk.

I said, " Well, I guess first... I'll pay off the credit cards bills and get rid of them." That felt like a wonderful relief... to say that I'd take care of them. Then I quietly celebrated with the others. My dream of winning money had come true in my dream... $100,000,000.00 True!

The evening before... I'd been thinking how wonderful it was... to have won money in my dreams. I've had many dreams of winning huge amounts of money. I love the thrill of the excitement... and the knowing that I'm holding the money in my hands. The feelings of winning are so real and intense in my dreams... they make you feel so good.

Actually these dreams of money refer to... dreams of things of value that I win... or recognize in life. In this dream... I felt relieved to pay off the debts... this means I'm clearing up the old and letting go... of the past debts or past issues of my life.

Sometimes money dreams seem to reflect... some accomplishments I have made. Winning can be as simple as recognizing... how I've grown within myself. When I'm out and about in the everyday world with other people... it's sometimes seems easier to see this... and recognize my accomplishments at that time. I don't shout them out... but they are still there... and I've won them by daring... to put my own thoughts out there to create my world.

Ex-Husband ♥

I was working on a project... but I can't really remember it. Then I'm walking into a large auditorium ... that's very crowded. Close to the front row... someone has saved a seat for me. I don't recognize anyone here... as I'm sitting close to the isle... and just watching the crowd. Then... I see two seats over is my ex-husband... with his cowboy hat on. At first we seem to be there separately... but then I realized we are together.

What ever the event is... it's not started yet... and there's no speaker. I ask the lady next to me, " Please save my seat... I need to use the restroom?" I go and when I return my seat is taken. I can still see all kinds of people... I don't recognize anyone and my ex is gone. The lady sees me... and half-heartedly apologizes about my seat. I feel disappointed and decide to leave. It's not really the place I want to be.

I now decide to go where... I know my ex is. I'm now walking on a sidewalk in a city block... that has lots of old tall oak trees. The trees are very green and vivid in color. It feels like this is a government property... and the buildings are federal property on this block.

Then I see my ex with a backpack... and he's stuffing it with money and gold bricks. I think we are in a building...but I'm not sure. He's just taking the money and gold... this feels like... it doesn't really belong to him. I now feel nervous... and want to get on our way. Next... we are now walking thru a large crowd of people. Everyone's pushing and shoving ...and we get separated. I do know where we are supposed to meet... so I go on ahead.

There is a woman there... who's an inspector and she's checking every one... since there maybe infiltrators within the government. I make it thru some shrubbery to the side of her... with only a little struggling to avoid her... and keep myself concealed. I'm concerned...I don't want anyone to know about... what my ex is smuggling out. Now... I'm in a large courtyard on the other side. There's beautiful green grass, more large oak trees... and still lots of people.

My dream shifts... and I see Mama San. She has one of my purple stained glass wind chimes... but it now has long strands of tiny bells... added to it. It is very light around her... and it feels like my bedroom that she's in ... and she's hanging it up for me.

Now... I'm back at the federal courtyard... and my ex is here. He has his money and gold in the backpack ... that he smuggled. Next... we are getting onto a greyhound bus to go home. I'm sitting in the front seat... watching the road ahead. The road is icy... but then it's turning to watery covered dirt. I'm wondering how long will it take...to get home ...to Las Vegas... because I know that's where this road leads.

The auditorium means a public place... but I also feel it may have something to do with my hearing. Mama San adding the tiny bells to my wind chime... represents my hearing too. Or maybe it's a message coming to me. I don't relate it to anything yet... in my life.

My ex husband is representative of an old outdated part of me. The smuggling of money refers to... misunderstood ideas... of where money comes from... and how it is created. The government refers to the laws of the universe... and we should use the universal laws when it comes to money. The crowds of people... are just that...everyone is searching for the truth in how to get money. The people also represent the many ideas... of where money comes from.

The road home isn't paved ...as its ice and dirt... this means my thoughts aren't stable yet. I need to pre-pave my path when it comes to creating the money. Know how the money is created... but I still need to follow thru with the right steps. The road to Las Vegas represents ... the road to wealth because that's what I associate with Las Vegas... wealth.

Gambling at the Pioneer ♥

I'm sitting over in the Video Keno area of the Pioneer Casino... actually I've been sleeping there. I was trying to get into my hotel room there... but it was late at night and it was not ready. All of a sudden... I realize... my purse has been stolen. I start calling for security... people gather around to see what's going on. A younger couple approach me. They tell me it would probably be faster... if I went up stairs to security to file a report. I agree and start walking... but the casino changes into a shopping mall.

Now I'm running thru isles inside the mall... trying to find my way to get to security. I can see the security office just over to the side of the hall way... but I can't get there. No matter how hard I try... I can't seem to get even close. Next it jumps... I have my purse back... but it's empty... all of my ID is gone too.

The casino represents my pleasure time... by sleeping I have not been paying attention. The room not being ready meant ... that I had not prepared myself. I needed to be more careful with my valuables (money) too... that was seen as my purse being stolen.

I knew what to do... as being represented by calling security. The shopping mall meant that I had choices... as to how I could make changes. But still I couldn't reach the security... or the changes I wanted to make. The empty purse made me feel that it was too late ...and I had lost myself... as well as my valuables (money.)

The money represented the things that which I held precious, dear and valuable... as well as the actual money itself... the good things in life. I wanted to make changes but didn't know how.

In my real life …I've been struggling on how to have more money thru prosperous ways of thinking…but this was more of a wake up call…sometimes it takes more than just thinking of prosperity. You need to be aware and get to the action part.

Get Your Own Towel ♥

I was with old girlfriends from a past way of life... which I did not care for. Then it switched and I was in East India. I was traveling... walking in the streets trying to find my way. All the girls and women seemed to have a lot of leaf green colored scarves and dresses. The whole market place and streets were very colorful.

I was searching and searching trying to find my way. I noticed I was all dusty and sweaty...I wanted to shower. I went into a palace... and asked a man if I could use the shower. He was in a maroon and gold dress with a turban on his head. He pointed to three shower stalls that had half doors of wood. He said " Yes, but you'll have to bring your own towel."

I started searching for a towel but couldn't find one anywhere...nor could I find anything to use in place of one. I decided to go back to the old past with the girlfriends and get one...which I did...then I returned to India to take my shower. Then I said to myself " Why did I need this towel at all? I could have drip dried."

Now the scene changes. I was an American...sitting on pillows and being served foods from a tray...like cheese and crackers. The East Indian girl serving me said " that will be $11.00, please." I said oh? I only had one dollar in my purse. As I looked in my purse...I had more money. I'd forgotten I had taken some money out of the bank. So, I handed the $11.00 to the girl next to me to give to her...but she ran away with the money. The server said " That will now be $45.00." I looked so puzzled that the girl serving said, " Well if you were one of us (meaning East Indian) it would only cost you 80 cents." For some reason... I got fearful and was running thru the streets...searching for the one who took my money.

The scene switched... I was standing in a kitchen in my new sky home (a house that I wanted to buy)... I'm looking at the kitchen floor, which were marble tiles... I had to go to the bathroom so much it hurt. So. I squatted behind the counter and went. Next, I see a little child like angel or cherub come in. He says " Oh, my." I said, " I couldn't help it and that I would clean things up."

I feel as thought I'm a time traveler in the dream. I am searching for new paths. I want to clean things up now... and from my past, too. By having to return to the past for a towel...I have to go back to where some of the things are that I want corrected now.

The shower meant... I wanted to clean off the old ideas and things of the past...returning to India to shower meant... I was looking to another wisdom to help change things.

The money aspect of different cultures represent... what we hold precious in one culture...is sometimes not the same value in another. Being from a country with different ways meant... I was expected to be able to pay more. Also, to me this represents that... I'm changing how I see my assets... or money ideas... thinking I have only a certain amount... when actually I've stored up more... or have more in my purse. I need to pay attention... that the wrong person...or thought doesn't take my assets.

Going to the bathroom in the house was a way of releasing... what I thought I'd wanted...but it wasn't the best house for me. I realized this when the angel appeared...then I said I'd clean it up.

It was very interesting...that the next day after this dream...was my birthday. I got a beautiful cobalt blue candleholder with an East Indian design of diamond mirrors around the bottom. I also got... $45.00 from a friend. I consider this a good coincidence...I only wish I did know when something meant... money is coming.

Gold Coins ♥

I'm an observer from somewhere... I can't see real scenery or myself. What I'm seeing are gold coins... in the air about one inch apart. They are in a steady stream... suspended in mid-air. Next... I see a gold leather purse in mid-air too. The gold color on the purse is dull almost plastic looking. Nothing else really happens here. I watch the gold coins... and I feel like want to take the coins... and put them inside the purse.

Then my dream seems... jumbled and moves from place to place. I'm at a work place in a casino. I'm with a couple of other women employees in an office. We are looking at two beautiful satin hand towels. The front of the towel is almost sheer... with small pink flowers on white... and the back is a regular white terry cloth. As the lady turns the towel over to the back... we can see they have flaws. The dye from the front had seeped thru... to the backside. One towel is darker pink in the back. I say, " they are still beautiful... and no one will notice." I want to know where they bought them... I want some too. Then I will get another towel for the woman... that's better made. They tell me they came from K-Mart.

It shifts... I'm now immediately at K-Mart... searching for towels. I ask someone... as I don't see them right away. I notice the store seems dark and over crowded with merchandise. I head up to a display at the checkout counter. I see the satin towels... all folded nicely... standing in a row. As I look... I don't see the flowered ones. I pull them up... one at a time to check them out. One has a small stuffed bunny in terry cloth... with a satin orange carrot... appliquéd to the satin towel. Another one has a beautiful raccoon on it. Most of the towels have animals on them...but no flowers. I leave and search at another counter... but no luck.

My dream jumps now... and I'm going home from work... but this is now Las Vegas, NV. I live in an apartment here in the city... but for some reason... I'm without a car. A lady co-worker offers to give me a ride. We are standing beside her SUV... and she has her young daughter with her. The lady says, " You know you'll need your keys... to get inside your apartment... even if you don't have a car." Then she tosses my set of keys to me. I don't feel so good about accepting the ride. I know I can make a decision. The city bus route is right near here... and I can take the bus. The bus means... I wouldn't feel obligated to her... and I can have the freedom of choice. I tell her, " I'll take the bus."

I walk a block or so over... and check the bus schedule. I've got an hour to wait. Then I notice there's a gym near by... that I had a membership to... I'll go there. As I walk in... the girls greet me and I hand them my card. I notice the expiration date on my card of 10-07-08. They decide to check the files of cards and update mine.

I'm looking around at the room... and the exercise equipment. I see massage chairs... about four of them. I'm thinking what a good place to start. Then as I sit down... the back and headrest fit perfectly to my body... its as if the chair adjust to you on its own. I can feel the relaxing massage on my neck... pulling out all the tension. I think I'll spend most of my waiting time here. Next... all the chairs are filled but one...but then it changes and there are eight chairs now.

I go to get my purse that I've placed at my feet... while I was in the chair. I see a woman lying underneath the chairs... and she's got my purse ... going thru it. I tell her that's mine and leave it alone...she just moves over to the next chair... and dumps the purse. I bend down to check my things... but I can't find my black wallet. I keep asking her, " Where is it? Where's my wallet?" She doesn't answer. I look thru the other stuff from my purse. I see small amethyst stones... and a small bag of gemstones... but no money... and my wallets still not there. I look and look... but its not there. I feel betrayed and disappointed.

I go outside and look around... I see a car wash. There's a young boy inside his fathers SUV. It's starting to go thru the car wash... but as the car wash pulls the SUV forward... the boy backs it up. This repeats several times. The boy then asks me... if I want a ride home... but I'm not sure. This doesn't feel good either. I don't accept his offer.

The dream changes now... and I've gone to collect some money a couple owe to me. They purchased something thru me... and I want to pay the bill. The couple is okay... and has most of the money to pay me. It's a very large sum of money. They start to ask if they can pay with a credit card instead of cash. Giving me the cash will take all their financial resources... the credit card would ease things.

The man pulls out a huge roll of cash... in the roll is a paper saying he's receiving a huge increase in pay. As I look at the money... I know I want to hold that money in my hands...the money feels good. At the same time... I know the money will pass from my hands to pay the bill I owe... where I had purchased that something they wanted for themselves. So... I say the credit card is okay... and we phone the information in from their credit card... and the bill gets paid.

It seems that I left there and went on my way... but I can't recall.

I'd been talking with a friend... the evening before the dream. We are both searching for ways... to have more money coming into our lives. We both seek financial prosperity... and financial freedom.

The gold coins represent money and money ideas. Since the coins were in mid-air that means... it's still in spirit... not in our physical world or physical purse. We are working in the right direction of increasing the money. The feeling of wanting to put the coins in the purse... refers to maybe we are a little anxious and don't want to wait.

When I don't accept the different rides home...this means I'm choosing... how to do what I want in life. I'm looking for the best ways... on my own. This is seen as... in the freedom I have when I take the bus.

My wallet being gone was an awful realization... that something precious and dear was missing. Not only does your wallet contain money... but your identification as well. I searched and searched... but couldn't find it. To me this represents the loss of my Mama San... who's now in the spirit world. She's very much a part of who I am... she's part of my identity. Loosing the wallet represents this... part of me has gone with her... and I can no longer find it.

I'm so grateful for the understanding... we are really only separated in the physical... but together in spirit always. In real life... I'd been blue for several days. I had not made the connection... because I'd thought I'd gotten past my loss. I guess I'm all too human... with emotions hidden deep inside... just like everyone else.

Then as I'm collecting the money from the couple for a debt means... a switching of ideas. I wanted the money... but took a credit card... and it went to pay the debt. I didn't get to keep the money anyway. The different forms of money... refer to...that which we hold dear, precious or valuable in our lives... and they are sometimes in different forms. The money and credit cards were interchangeable... but not quite the same. It's like us... part human (physical) and part spirit ...sometimes interchangeable... but not quite the same.

Hundreds of Hundreds ♥
(Name Sake Dream)

I see tall green mountains in the background. As I start to look closer around me... I see tall pine trees... but where I'm standing... it is like dried brush. I'm looking over at a stream that comes down from the mountains. It feels like the wilderness of the old west. I am a Native American Indian girl of about 20 years. I'm dressed in a light colored buckskin dress... with long fringe and a few beads. My hair is long, black and in a single braid down my back.

I've come for a walk away from the village. I wanted some peace and to be with nature. There's a lot of strife in our camp. Times seem to be hard and... not enough food to go around. Everyone is edgy. I'm just walking ... looking at the earth and the rocks, the dry brush. I'm wondering why things change so much... and sometimes not in ways for the better. It's very quiet here... I hardly hear a sound... and I don't see any animals.

I'm thinking... if I just had it in my power... I'd create abundance for everyone. But in my heart... I know it doesn't work that way. Other people have to want the abundance you'd create for them... or their thoughts only cancel it out. I talk to the Great Spirit... back and forth we talk. I know he hears and understands.

Just then... there's a wind swirling around my feet... and I'm off balance and I fall. I quickly get up to see what it was. I look over to a dry meadow... and I see some spotted ponies staring at me... or at least I think its me... but behind me is a swirling wind. I run to the stream... near a tree thinking I'll be safe. Then loud as thunder I hear a voice... and it says, " Look in the stream." I look around wondering who said that… maybe it was the wind? Again I hear, " Look in the stream."

It jumps a little in the dream…because I'm standing in the dark blue water of the stream. I can see the rocky shore… and a tree branch that has fallen into the water. I see myself in my buckskin dress and my long braid …and I'm wading in the water. I'm looking but I don't see anything. Then its like I hear the voice… and its much softer… like coming from inside me. It says, " To look into the stream within a stream… and I'll find what I'm looking for."

I decide to look in the water. As I put my face into the water and open my eyes… I see only a blur. Then it clears a little… and I see a tiny goldfish… he must be only ½ inch long. He's cute… and I think what could he do to help me? Then in the background I see… hundreds of hundreds of them… all shiny bright gold in the blue water of the stream.

I stand up to catch my breath and as I do… the little fish swims into my hand. Suddenly… there's a flash of light… and he changes into a huge trout… almost big enough to feed the whole village. WOW! I feel so happy… I hurriedly take the fish over to where the spotted ponies are. I start cleaning it …and getting ready to cook the fish. I hear the voice say, " You can come anytime and the little fish will help you… your people can accept this." How wonderful this is… and it feels so good.

The dream changes… and I'm a pioneer girl… dressed in a pale yellow long dress with a huge flowery bonnet. My father recently died and I'm all alone… wondering how am I going to make it?

I strangely recognize the stream I'm standing near. Next, I just walk into the water clothes and all. Then suddenly there are all these tiny goldfish all around me. There must be hundreds of hundreds of them. One swims into my hand… and in a flash of light… he changes into a $100.00 bill. I'm so amazed… I let four or five of the swim into my hand… and they change into $100.00 bills. I feel so happy… I know that even while I'll miss my father… the little fish will help me.

I hear in my heart… to always look to the stream within the

stream… whatever you need is there. The little fish will change into what ever you need… they are happy to serve… and remember there are always hundreds of hundreds of them.

    The Indian girl is a part of me… that is older in wisdom. The wisdom is shown by her wanting to create for the whole village…and by the understanding that… she has to allow them each… their own creation. The tiny fish seemed like the magic of the universe. The little fish gave other options to the people… that they could use… and could understand.

    The second part of the dream… is like a remembrance of the first part. I need to look in the stream that's inside the stream… refers to looking for the higher expectations in the spiritual waters of life. Look inside myself for what I desire… and the little fish change to serve my desires.

Ice Cream Man ♥

I'm living in a desert city… when I get a notice to go to work for the post office. I show up at a large post office. I know it's the town I now live in… but as I'm looking at the post office… its about two acres big in size. It looks like a massive sorting plant. There's a girl with me… and she hands me a time card. We start walking thru this massive scene… of machinery and people until we reach a central area. We clock in and another lady starts to show us where we'll work. It's noisy and very confusing… but each worker seems to know his or her job.

She takes me… to where the carriers are. They are standing inside of a huge sorting machine. I can see wires… that are like inside a circuit board going overhead… and then all around each carrier. They pull down a chute to get their mail. It's like the sorting machines they have now… but each carrier is inside of his station or route… that sits within the machine.

My job is to hand sort the letters… that don't fit into the sorting slots. I'm watching as a carrier pulls down the chute… and some government checks are falling into a tray. I start to say, " These mostly look like checks." He thinks I said, " All the checks"… and starts filling tray after tray. I'm trying quickly to sort them now… as I know I need to get back to the time clock. I feel overwhelmed… because I'm not trained yet.

It jumps… and I'm at the time clock searching in the slots for my time card. The girl I came with is there too. As I finally find my card… it's crumpled… but I use it and clock in anyway. A woman supervisor starts yelling at me… that I was late coming back from a break. She wants me to clock in and out at break time now. I don't say anything... but when the post office plant is two acres in size... it takes all your break time to walk to one central time clock.

She continues to yell at me... as we start leaving to sort letters in a distribution case. She tells another worker to let me have her seat... plus I'll be working at the other station... that is next to the worker. " Just pull the seat over there," she says. As I do... and I start to adjust the seat... it's half buried in the ground. The floor is partially gone... and the chair or seat is two feet under the ground.

The scene changes and I'm looking for a house to rent... since I have the post office job in this town now. I see a sort of log cabin style place. The man there says he's moving...and I can rent it... so I do. I'm in my new house... but it feels lonely inside... its not a pretty house or anything special... just a house.

Then I'm wondering about my Mama San... and how she is... since she's not here with me. I remember seeing a small cabin out back ...of the place I rented. I go inside and there's Mama San. She says, " I've been here all along." I'm so happy to see her. I'm next wondering... if she'll be comfortable here. I see only part of a gold curtain on a window... and the place is very small. She walks with me... and we look at the kitchen. It's painted white... and it's only the size of a closet. I see a very tall white fridge... that's slender and small... next to the cabinet. Mama San says it's okay... and we'll get things arranged... so it's easy to use. We talk for a while... then I need to leave.

I'm going to work... when the man I rented the house from... says he's like to have it back. I tell him, " I'm not sure." He says you can't believe some of the places there are to rent in this town... they're awful. I know he wants me to trade places with him. He takes me to the entrance of his apartment. All I can see is rows of windows... mostly broken... in an old brick building... with no porches or steps. It really looks more like the alleyway.

He then reaches inside a broken pane of glass... and flips a switch to unlock the door. As we go in... I immediately see stairs going up. The walls are dirty dusty bricks... and a part of the stairs is brick too. He's ahead of me... telling me about the place. I tell him, " My Mama San can't walk up any stairs "... as she'll be coming with me... but he continues on talking. I now see avocado green shag carpet everywhere... even partially on the stairs. As I look up... I get a view of the whole apartment building. It's one big roof over the apartments... and the apartments all have open ceilings to the one roof. Not only that... the roof inside is that green carpet... next I see the walls to each apartment are green carpet too.

I don't like it here... and I start to tell him that... when he says another friend lives there too...this male friend now joins us. I excuse myself to use the bathroom. When I go in... I see the toilet is a large open stone pit... with a water source at one end. It's a community toilet. This is not the place for me... and I leave. Then I'm back with the man and I'm telling him... this is not the kind of place I'd live in... and I certainly couldn't bring Mama San there.

He says they (he and his friend) will give me a ride back to my house. At first... I'm in the front seat with him... and his friend is in the back seat. Then it switches... they are in the front seat... and I'm in the back... and the man's girlfriend is sitting next to me. I have on a silky gray fur jacket. The girl asks, " What's that on your jacket?" As I look down... I see it's a piece of white fur from my cat. I tell her it's only cat hair... and I start to pull it off... but some of the gray fur comes off too. Now there's a big chunk of fur and they stop the car. They are asking me... what I'm going to do with it? As I look out the car window... see green plants in an open field and I see some birds. I tell them... I'll toss it out... and the birdies will use it for nesting material.

The scene switches... the man is now standing in the field... and has a large spotted goose on a leash. The goose is trying to get closer to the fur. Then several odd colored birds... start approaching the piece of fur too. Some are pink with brown spots... some are grayish and white... but each sort of looks like a goose. They each want to eat the piece of fur.

Now we are back in the car... and the girl wants to go to her house. As we drive along... the guys decide to stop at a place to visit a friend. When I look at the person's house... it's not a house... but a piece of open desert property... with the insides of a house... just sitting there on the ground. It's all in the open. I see a bathroom vanity sitting in an open field... then table and chairs in another part. It looks so odd.

Then ...I hear the girl get out of the car... and slam the door. She's mad. She wants to get home... and she starts walking. As she gets to her house... I'm looking at it with her. It's brown and... made of wood and stone. On the ground level... there's a porch leading to the door... but the wooden planks are missing. You can see straight down into a stone basement. You can't enter into the house. I walk to the side of the house... and it has large windows. It's really a log cabin style house... but there is no way to get in. Then I notice the house is very small... actually too small to fit over that large basement.

The scene jumps... and another close friend of mine has joined us... and all of us are back... at the first man's apartment. My new friend has brought ice cream bars with him. At first... I see four chocolate covered bars... and I hand them out to our friends. Then I see three other bigger ice cream bars appear... and three other people show up. Again I see four more large ice cream bars appear inside a bag. We all eat one... and everyone is content. It seems as though they were very hungry... when we arrived at the apartment.

The dream scene changes again. The five of us... my newest friend, the two guys, the man's girlfriend and myself... we are all at a casino. I see my friend in his black tee shirt... playing a slot machine. I'm talking with the girlfriend...when one of the guys comes up... and says my friend hit a big jackpot.

As I look at my friend in the black tee shirt... I see silver dollar coins spewing into the air. I walk over and ask what did he hit. He says '1875.' I look at the red numbers on the screen of the slot machine... and it says '1875'... but I'm thinking it has to be

Dreams: The Money Jars

$18,750.00... it's a dollar machine. Everyone is so excited. My friend just smiles... and keeps playing the machine next to it... while he's waiting to get paid his jackpot.

My dream was very vivid and detailed... and it refers to... some old ideas and past things I'm going over. In each part... I can relate to past events.

At the post office and my job... this refers to a past way of working thru life. In my real life ...I've chosen to go on to something else. I think that's why the building was so huge... and why the supervisor yelled at me. Things have changed in this respect for me. If I do choose to work there... my seat is buried in the earth... and so am I.

Then I search for a house to rent... this means looking at suitable parts of myself... if I did choose to work at the post office. The place I chose is just okay... and doesn't provide the elements of happiness and growth. When I'm concerned about Mama San... she represents my older female creativity and wisdom. She is always there with me... as she says she is... but she's cramped into this house too. We want to go on in our growth and happiness... not just accept another job or place.

Next... the friend has decided he wants his old place back... this represents returning to a past way of life... and since the friend is really a part of myself... I'm not sure I want this. His apartment maybe okay... but it wasn't a step forward... and I didn't want to switch or go backwards.

Then... as I travel with the friends in the car... it's like going along with an association of ideas... as we explore places in life. Seeing the open house in the desert... is like viewing different possibilities in the things we choose. The girlfriend's house was incomplete... because you couldn't get to the door. It has a good strong basement... which means the foundation from inside the earth was in place...but the outside building was small and unfinished. This idea that she represents... needs to grow some more to become complete.

Mary Belle Claude

The man with the goose on the leash… that tries to eat the cats fur means… that some parts of us are hungry for the enlightenment in life… and we'll stretch our leash as far as we can… to get even a taste of it. This is seen too… by my close friend visiting and we are eating the ice cream bars. It's like eating the cream of life.

Then my friend winning the jackpot… this represents a positive part of myself… that has won things of value in my life. This is very true in my real life… as I've made better financial choices… and I did win… and gain new ideas and things of value.

♥

Irish Dream ♥

My dad of this life time and I were going on a trip to Ireland. Once there...we were surprised at how laid back the people were. They seemed so happy and calm about everything...but we did notice they drank a lot of ale or beer...and spent very little time working. It seemed everything was always done and things kept up.

We were in a small pub that had a casino in it. I was playing a 5 cent or nickel machine. I hadn't played long and I hit a jackpot. There was a large bucket beneath the slot machine...that just kept filling up...and filling up. I had to get another bucket. Then I noticed... I'd hit a 200,000-nickel jackpot or $10,000.00. I heard an Irish woman in the back ground say "Wouldn't you know it...a foreigner got it. I play that machine all the time."

As I collected my jackpot...I saw a huge oval metal bathtub in the bar area... it had ice water and cold beer. The bartender was adding more to it. He said " It's a custom round here to buy everyone in the casino a drink...when you hit the big one." I seemed to agree...but watched my jackpot go down.

Then there was a big celebration parade...my dad and I joined in. Everyone had on large ribbons and sashes...as they danced in the street...with their ale in one hand, of course. It was so joyous and happy. After the dance we could choose each others ribbons and by doing this we chose our mates, husbands and wives. One particular woman...who was very nice and pretty wanted my dads ribbons. I felt this was great...since my dad had been lonely after my mother's death. I helped her get the ribbons...they seemed so happy.

I decided to go to my room to rest because I felt tired. As I lay on the couch... some one on the next floor up was sweeping... and the dust kept falling in my face and eyes. I yelled " Hey, look at this." I could see the dust flying all around.

Then it switched...my dad and I were in America... getting things ready so we could return to Ireland to live. I felt happy...but was still concerned about all the drinking...I decided to try it.

A man I seem to recognize as a boyfriend approached me. Most of the feelings of the relationship 'boyfriend' was that he wanted me...but I had no particular interest or feelings for him. He seemed angry and defiant most of the time. I told him that I was going...that if he wanted to come with us to try it...he could.

Then there was a time shift in the dream. I was dressed in a beautiful lacy Victorian dress. It was pale rose and pale green strips with lots of ruffles. I had a lot of petticoats and a bustle...and a very large beautiful bonnet of the same material. I was in a public bathhouse and I was sitting in an old large porcelain tub... that was filled with warm soapy water...with all my clothes on. Then this so called boyfriend came in...and started attacking me...while I was in the tub. I screamed " Rape! " Immediately, people pulled him off me.

Now, I'm back in Ireland with my dad...he's happy getting settled in with his new wife. I'm walking down a road almost floating above it... there beside me is a nice tall man...with black hair and a black top hat. We are having a lot of fun going our way...on the road. Then there's a large dip in the road and...I felt off center for a moment...then I was back.

The scene changes ... I could see someone holding up a large yellow ticket or note... it was in front of me...beyond that I could see rolling green hills and trees...there were small cottages and farms everywhere. It was so peaceful here. The note said there was a current pesticide chemical that had been in use. It had been recalled because it caused dangerous side effects. Instead of everyone getting a notice... a town meeting was called in the valley. In the meeting, everyone was told of the note...as I sat there I wrote notes about the recall in my notebook. The people thought this was strange because...they had the ability to recall any thought...to remember it...and also to think as a group mind.

Next... someone was showing movies on the side of a barn. We were still in this green valley... and it was daylight. The charge for the movie was quarter...but several people sat in their chairs to the side... without paying since it was outside anyway...no one seemed to mind.

Then I'm sitting at a table and there's a man across from me. He's showing me papers about what he owns. He said " this is my dowry for you, it's worth $80,000.00." It seemed okay... but I really wasn't interested or had feelings for this man. Then in an instant it changed...someone beside me says " it's too late... the man is dead." Next, someone is showing me lots of deeds and titles to lands...that this man owns. I wasn't sure how to feel except I was sad.

In the Irish dream, moving from one country to another means... I'm changing my state of awareness. My dad... being with me is the older male positive wisdom... who is with me... and a part of me at the same time.

Winning in the casino was great... it meant... I'm winning at successfully changing my awareness. The old boyfriend represents a part of me...that tried to cling on after I'd made the decision to change (or move to Ireland.)

A few days after this dream... I found out that it is true... the choosing of someone's ribbons is a custom in some of the European countries. I'd never heard of it before. My dad remarrying represents a balance in that older wisdom... as male and female reunite.

I'm following my new chosen path... as seen by the tall man and myself going along the road. New ideas are being presented to me... this is represented as the village meeting of the people... with their way of thought processing.

I think the man with the dowry represented a positive idea for me… and the dowry is what I gain if I chose this path. But the man died… meaning the concept or idea wasn't really ready…or I wasn't ready…it was gone before I had a chance to accept it.

Leisure Time – Dog in the Box ♥

I'm in a casino on Fremont Street in Las Vegas. It's an older casino… I can tell by the décor and the small size. I'm walking around looking for a slot machine to play. I can see large windows to the front… and dark carpet on the floor. My friend is there with me… but I don't see him… he's playing in another area.

I'm watching… as some of my favorite machines are removed… and are now sitting to one side. They've left only a few of the older favorites. People are wanting to play them… but its limited seating. I'm taking out some money… from a small black coin purse to play on. I'm now sitting at a machine… I don't really recognize the game I'm playing. Its just okay and I don't seem to be winning much.

Next it switches… I'm lying on the floor… next to a curved black railing…near a bi-level section of the casino. Its quiet here and I'm sleeping. It feels really good to sleep and rest. I'd put my back next to the railing … so that I felt protected and safe. My friend walks up to me and says, " Wake up." I'm groggy but coming out of my sleep. Then as I'm still there and… I have my cat 'Sushi' with me… and she's curled up in my arms with her head under my chin. Sushi's asleep and she doesn't want to wake up… she's content to be there to be with me.

Then… I'm walking back to somewhere in the casino…but the scene is different. I see a river in front of the casino. Several older men are playing slot machines. I go to get some money from my purse... and I pull out some $20.00 bills and a $10.00 bill. I see the clear green color of the money. It looks so vivid... and feels good. I start counting... as to the amount I brought... and what I have spent. I say, " That's right... I brought a hundred dollars with me... and I have a lot left."

I decide to go to the restroom. A couple of other women are there. We wash up and leave. The restroom was kind of messy... but it was okay.

Next...everything completely changes now. I'm going into a dimly lit garage. There are no windows... and the walls are unfinished and dusty. Boxes, old bikes and other stuff are just lying around. I see myself inside this garage... but I'm in a collapsible black plastic mesh automobile. It feels like the car is my body. Its like I'm driving around inside the garage.

I see an old slot machine... and I want to take the money out of it. It feels like everything here has been abandoned. I take the money... and put it in my purse... as I do I get a weird feeling... and notice something. That something is... an old wooden box, covered in dust and lint... but more than that... it's a security device to protect the garage. Actually... there's a mechanical dog inside the box. I feel it's watching me... but at the same time it's okay. I have my arm on the car door of my collapsible mesh car... and as I look down... and see a piece of burlap over the security box. Then I see the wet nose of the mechanical dog... thru the burlap.

As I decide to leave and start to back out of the garage... a kid on a bike rides in. He says, " Is that really a car?" I say, " yes"... and as I pull out onto the street the car collapses... then I'm peddling it like a bike. The kid has disappeared... and I'm now walking back to the casino...and no more car.

Then as I'm walking... I look down at the ground... and its covered in large red ants. The ants are carrying seeds and leaves. As I go to move one foot in front of the other...the ants run out in front of my feet. I'm careful not to step on them. For a long time in my dream I stay here... I'm just watching my feet...every time I move them... the red ants run ahead of my footsteps...each time.

Dreams: The Money Jars

I'm so fascinated … I just keep watching.

In this dream… I can look back to the day before and see where my mind pulled the information from… then used it… to make the dream story.

I'd been watching the ants in my yard… the old garage was at my friend's place…and another friend and I were talking about the casino.

In the casino…as my friend is playing in a different area this means… he's doing his own thing. This relates to… what each of us is really doing… our own thing in life. The casino represents… a fun filled exciting place in my leisure time… in dreams and in real life.

The older machines being removed means… some of my ideas of having fun are changing. What was a favorite… no longer appeals to me… its outdated. Then I'm sleeping with my cat on the casino floor… this means… I'm resting and re-evaluating my choices in entertainment. I'm also re-evaluating my choices with money. I count it out from my purse … then I'm recognizing… it's the richness I create that brings the enjoyable leisure time.

The old garage represents… an old part of me where things are stored and I want to retrieve some items of value… the money. Next… I'm in the collapsible car… this means things are changeable in my body… this is true in real life… I'm on a healing program. The dog in the box represents… there's an ever faithful part of myself… that watches over me… no matter what I'm doing… even if it does feels weird.

I was so intrigued with the ants in the dream… and watching them go before my feet…is like watching life. I do feel very intrigued… as I watch other people and the things they create in their lives… then they go on about their business.

Two weeks after this dream… my friend from the dream and I went on a trip to the casinos. At Whiskey Pete's… all our old favorite keno machines had been removed. We were disappointed and the next day we drove into Las Vegas. Downtown at our favorite casinos... The Golden Gate had removed their machines completely. The Las Vegas Club had only a hand full... and the Western Hotel only six left. It seems that... an era had ended for us. The old feeling of excitement was gone...without our favorite machines being there. I did come home with a $100.00 bill in my purse. I didn't know how much the dream foretold ...of the changes that had been made... until we were there.

Millions Clearly Stated ♥
(Name Sake Dream)

I'm living near a crowded city with lots of tall buildings. A short distance from my apartment... is lots of law and court buildings. I've just received an official notice... to appear in one of the oldest courts with the most judicial power of all. It's in a very tall old building... that's always over crowded with people trying to get to their places.

This day... I'm standing in my bath... deciding what to wear for my court appearance. I want my light blue suit... but I hear in my head. " Wear the navy blue one... as this place means lawful business...you need to be properly dressed." I've planned for a taxi... to get me there about one hour ahead of time. I feel good ...although a little nervous... because I don't really know what the summon is for.

It's slightly rainy as I arrive... and there seem to be twice as many people as usual. I pay the taxi and head inside. This old building has only stairs... to get from one level to the next... and it must be forty stories tall. I look at the main stairway... there are so many people clinging to each other... shoving and pushing each other. They are practically dangling from the stair edges. I think how will I ever get up there... to the top to keep my appointment time. I need help... all the stairways look the same.

As I step back... over to the right... I see a glass elevator. Its as if no one else sees it... no one is around. There is a porter standing there at the elevator. I can see he has on a navy blue double-breasted suit... with gold buttons. There seems to be a soft golden glow of light around the glass elevator. He's smiling at me... and even the buttons on his suit seem to glow. No one else see this elevator? I decide this is definitely for me. As I step inside I ask, "What is this?" He says, "It's the secret." I feel very good to be here... and I know I'll reach my destination.

As the glass door opens at the top floor... its still crowded. I thank the porter and head into the room. I see my friend...who is an attorney. He's offered to be with me. The courtroom is so busy... people in cubicles everywhere... trying to get their business done. In the center of the room is a tall podium... and there sits the judge... in his black robe... with the gavel in his hand...looking very authoritarian.

I hear the session called to order... and his gavel hit's the desk. He's calling out my name... and the names of several attorneys representing the case. He's asking if all the paper work is in order? Now, about three of four attorneys approach the bench. I can't hear what they are saying... but several minutes pass.

Next... the judge is reading off a list of assets... he's naming properties...stock market investments... a couple of prominent successful business... even the names of several books... and a bank account with the balance of over $550,000,000.00 - five hundred fifty million dollars!

Then he calls me to the bench... I feel a little nervous. He states my name... then says, " as I have stated these are now yours. Its millions clearly stated... and you are the owner...everything is properly in order. Its yours!" I feel a rush of joy and excitement. Everyone is smiling. I feel so happy inside. The judge hit's the gavel on the desk... and stands up to leave. All the attorneys are smiling and happy for me. It's mine!

The secret elevator got me there... I now have everything I've wanted. It's mine!

WOW!! Wouldn't it be so nice! In real life! The crowded city means... the crowded ideas of the world and of civilization. I'm finding my way to the natural laws of the universe... and understanding how to create what I want... using these laws.

Dreams: The Money Jars

Everyone hanging and clinging to the stairs to get to the top... is like holding on to the old ideas and ways... of where money comes from. The glass elevator that takes me to the top is the secret... which to me represents the book I have been reading...'The Secret.' It has help me tremendously in my life and in my understanding.

The courtroom represents... these natural laws of the universe. As I put my new knowledge into action... I'm summoned to court...where these laws abide. I'm learning to put things in order... this is seen when the judge ask if everything is in order. He states this again at the end also... after the documents are read... everything is in order.

Then the most wondrous part is when... the judge states the fantastic wealth and money belong to me... its mine! Of course... in real life this dream... just plain feels good... and is awesome in its self. But the meaning I've realized... is that I deserve this wealth and money... just by asking... it is there. All things are possible... if we use the right laws of the universe. WOW !!! I want to see this one in real life!

New Credit Cards ♥

I'm going into a casino... although I can't determine why... if its to play or work? Next to me... is a younger attractive woman... and we are walking into the entrance. When we are inside... it's huge... but I don't see it clearly. What I do notice is... the woman is very flighty. She stops at one place... then jumps to another. Her energy level is good... but not stable... and the same for her thoughts. I'm thinking to myself, " Why is she with me?"

I play a few slot machines... but it's really more of a show... watching her. We are walking toward an elevator... at the back of the casino. As we start to step up to it... the scene then switches...there's now a whole room that surrounds the elevator. As I look around... it's the security department of the casino.

I see the security room divided into four sections... with accounting areas, offices and camera surveillance departments. The ceiling is very low here... and it congested with all the employees. There are lots of men in suits ...and several men in dark blue security uniforms.

As I look toward the elevator... that's now at the back of that room... there's a soft light coming from it. I'm thinking... we must have been looking for the light of the elevator... and not paying attention to where we walked. I'm now telling this to... a man in a suit... that's part of the security department... who wants to know why we are here.

While all this has been going on... the woman who's with me... started to walk in... but is backing up. She sees a machine for imprinting credit cards... on her way out. The machine has blank cards... and no one is around that area. So she stops... and is printing out credit cards for herself. She has a whole handful... of new credit cards in her name. I'm thinking, " How wonderful... just print them yourself." Suddenly... she walks away... to get a different type of credit card to print. When she returns to print more... she gets a couple done... then a security man is telling us to leave.

We now walk over to a huge escalator. Its dark in this part of the scene... almost black around the escalator. I can only see a small amount of light on it. It's like the escalator is traveling... in the black of unknown space... because I see no walls... just the escalator.

We want to go to our rooms... and we know the escalator is safe in getting us there. As we step on... the woman says she's so tired... she can't stay awake and she falls asleep. Then... its like I'm an observer in the distance. I see the shiny metal escalator going up and around... like a Ferris wheel. The woman is peacefully sleeping... on its steps... while it travels around and around... no one bothers her.

As the escalator is getting close to the top... some security guards have become aware of the woman. At first they are just watching her sleep... and commenting on her sexy clothes... and that her blouse is open. Next...they are waking her up... and helping her to the room.

The scene switches... I've been asked to help one of my brothers... at his work place. I really don't want to do this. I'm walking in a small building... that sells something... I'm not sure what it is. I'm getting my cash drawer ready... and I put some keys in it.

The keys are on a shiny silver ring... and I'll be able to unlock something quickly... if a customer asks for it. My brother says no... and puts the keys in a different drawer... closer to what it unlocks. That makes sense... if its closer to what it unlocks. But now... the drawer looks more like a shiny toolbox... and there are more tools in the drawer.

It jumps a little... I see a man on a very small Ferris wheel that has tiny seats. He's trying to ride it... but he is bigger than the ride. Then I have a flashback... I see the same man... and he's jumping out of an airplane... parachuting in a dark sky. He's doing it over and over. He says... he can't get enough of the thrill. But now... something has changed ... he's bigger than the ride he chose. I wonder... how will he recapture the thrill on such a small Ferris wheel?

The dream was long and very detailed. It was like a long movie... that skipped around a lot. The dream represents... that I'm entering into a new part of myself. The woman who is flighty... is a part of me in new stages of growth. That's why she seems to jump around a lot.

Then we are headed to the elevator means...we are going up to higher ideas. We then get side tracked by not paying attention... to where we are at the time... and end up at security. This means we still must observe the natural laws... while we are learning.

The woman represents... the new creative part of myself. She prints up new credit cards... this is like making sure whatever... is needed on our path is available. If you need credit ...just print it up. It's like having thoughts of abundance and prosperity... and putting those ideas forth. So that it is made manifest... and it is there to use.

The escalator going up... makes me feel like my life is traveling upwards... to new goals and new ambitions. Since the woman is sleeping on the escalator... I think I'm not fully aware of all things... that are bringing me to the top. I have the security guards watching me... which means... the laws of the universe guide me and my journey... and they are keeping me safe.

The last part of the dream... has to do with volunteer work... I was asked to do in real life. I declined the work... as I didn't want to do it. The keys represent... there are keys to the work place... if I want to get closer to working a job. But it's volunteer work... no pay... just like the man trying to ride the tiny Ferris wheel... hoping to find a big thrill of the real thing... like parachuting out of a plane.

Poker Chips ♥

I'm over in the table area at a cocktail bar… that's older and seedy. The bartender is nice and it seems pleasant. I start to sit down with some friends at a wooden table…we have our drinks in hand. On one side of the table are chairs…but I chose the side with a bench.

As I slide in… about half the way down… two women approach us… insisting that the bench is theirs. I call the bartender over to settle the dispute. He says it's my seat. Then the two women change… into an older lady and her husband. She gets really angry and says… she doesn't have to stay here. The husband is just watching her… as she walks behind the bar to a counter. There is a huge round wheel of poker chips… the chips look mostly white. She states " Well, these are mine… so I'm taking them with me." As she grabs them… she drops most all of them on the floor… because she's drunk and unsteady. The husband now helps her pick them up … and they leave.

As I'm standing watching …the scene changes a little. It seems as though… there is now a very handsome man standing there. He is in a very nice satin black suit… asking me to dance. I almost feel as if… he has something to do with the woman and the poker chips… or money. I really like him… I feel a bond of closeness. We dance for a long time. Then a male friend of his… who's wearing a tan suit… approaches us. My friend and I are embraced… our arms around each other… we are standing side by side… talking to his friend. Then I notice… his friends' nice suit has lint and fuzz all over it.

The dream scene jumps…the three of us are in a courtroom.

The proceedings have something to do with the bar... and the earlier incident of the women and the poker chips. I'm walking over to sit down... my new friend and I sit at a bench together... there's a soft light around us. Next to us is an older lady... with beige blonde hair... who looks very wealthy. The friend in the tan suit is on the other side of the wealthy woman. The woman smiles at me... as if to say... everything will be okay.

    The cocktail bar is a place of worldly entertainment. This means that... I'm out there in the world watching the entertainment...and learning to make my choices. The women (creative ideas) are insisting the bench belongs to them... that means... some ideas want to replace others or to be recognized...but maybe they aren't the best ideas. I have the choice of intervention by the bartender... that I can ask his help. He represents a positive outlook... he's the peacekeeper.
    The angry woman with the poker chips is a part of myself. Maybe I'm trying to hard to hold onto something. One of the women (creative ideas) changes to the husband...and that means a balancing of ideas for the angry woman. The man that dances with me... also means a balancing of myself. The male & female aspects... the positive & creative aspects... that balance life.
    The biggest message of this dream for me is... you can't force the money to come to you... its like being the angry woman. You must go thru the process of natural laws... which is what the courtroom represents. The wealthy lady being in the courtroom where proceedings take place... represents this, also. Then the money and wealth... will come easily and naturally.
    It is true... I'm been trying too hard to increase money in my life. I should work at things in a different light...with more of a balancing of my ideas... not forcing my ideas.

Roman Coins ♥

I dreamed... I was sleeping in my bed. I was tossing and turning... trying to get comfortable. The scene is dark were I am... and I don't recognize anything but my bed. My bed feels hard... so I decide to get up and look at it... to see what's going on. I'm not sleeping anyway.

As I pull back the covers... the bed is a piece of... one-inch thick hard plywood... no padding at all. Then I decide to look under my bed to see what's supporting it. As if by magic... I'm standing below a tall tree with large branches... no leaves just branches.

I'm looking up in the tree... at the piece of plywood... over a tree branch. My bed is in a tree. Beneath the wood is a couple of long shiny steel pipes... like water pipes... that give it support... if it were on the ground... but it's in a tree. I then notice one piece of pipe is a leg to the bed... about three feet long... but there's only one leg... and its just sticking out there in mid-air. Now... I'm really wondering... how do I sleep at all... in a wooden bed on a tree branch ...suspended in mid-air?

Next... I'm looking around... its pleasant here... where I'm standing on the earth. It feels very light and open...but somehow it feels... unusual. As I look down... the ground is almost glowing. I see large round plate-sized pieces of... light colored terra cotta clay. The whole ground is covered in these very light...almost white terra cotta earthen disks. There's a soft mist...like fog coming up from the ground... and the earth is glowing... it's a mystical feeling. It feels like Rome. I don't see any buildings... only a few sparse trees.

I have a walking stick in my hand... and I'm walking around. As I look down... I see a large gold coin in the center of one of the disk. It's loose in the plate disk... so I pry it up. The gold coin is solid gold... and larger than a silver dollar. The front of the coin... has the imprint of a Roman Goddess... and the back has some symbols. When I pull out the coin... there's another coin beneath. I take it out and there's another coin. I end up with four solid gold coins.

I feel so good ...and where I am... feels really good and peaceful... that I'm just walking around here ...and look thru the mist and the soft light for a long time in my dream. Then... I'm looking at more of the earthen disk... and I see a gold coin as big as a dinner plate. As I pry it up... it's very beautiful...solid gold with the Goddess... on the front of it. But for some reason... I decide it's too heavy to carry... and I lay it back down. I decide to leave it for some else. Now... I see a man in the distance with a walking stick too. He's searching in the mist for the earthen plates... with the coins inside. I take only what I can carry... at this time.

My bed represents... a place where I rest, sleep and dream. It's where I retreat from the world... and where my unconscious world begins. Since my bed is up in a tree this means... that the unconscious part of myself... is up over the physical world. But for some reason I'm not comfortable... the bed is hard.

In real life... I've be saying to myself... that it should be easier to over come the past... and even more easier to create... my new future... that I want to achieve. Maybe my unconscious mind... is repeating the message in the dream. I do seem to have struggled with some changes.

Once I am awake... and I notice my earthly place... that seems so mystical, peaceful and beautiful...and I am aware of myself again. Then when I see the things I want to achieve... and they appear like magic... this is the golden coins.

For me the golden coins represent two things. The first is my books I'm writing... and second is the wealth and abundance... I want to achieve in this life. The one coin coming after another means…each thing I'm achieving will led on to even more. I feel this is very true for me.

Why I didn't keep the biggest gold coin of all… is a little baffling. Especially since wealth and money… are a big part of things I want to experience. I think the man searching for the coins also… may represent a friend…who has helped me with my books being published. I may have left the large coin for him. It was my gold coin to take… but maybe I need to grow more… so that the coin isn't so heavy.

The Band ♥

I'm standing on a street corner in a large city. All the buildings are tall and crammed together. As I look up... there is light in the sky...but you can't see much of it. It's almost as if there is a clear glass... over the top of the buildings connecting them ... it feels like a glass atrium room.

I go into a place that turns out to be a music club. Lots of people are waiting to see a certain band. The members of the band come out one at a time... each dancing frantically around and announcing his name. The names are unusual...one particular name I remember was ' Ham- Burg.' He's a nice looking European fellow...with dark hair.

Listening to the music is okay... but it doesn't feel all that good here ...and it's crowded...plus I don't know anyone. I want to go up to my room. I walk out to the street... but all I can see is more buildings with doors. I don't recognize any of these places. As I walk thru a set of doors... it's not the right place... to get to where I want to go. I do this several times ...and then I feel exhausted. I go back towards the club... and I see Ham-Burg. I tell him my situation...and I ask for his help... and he says, " Sure I'll help you." He calls one of his buddies over...next we are walking towards the back of a street... by the club. I now see... two large shiny clear glass doors. They each open the doors for me... as I go inside. I say thank you for showing me the way to my room... this is where I want to be.

Later, I go out ...and I'm walking down a city path... that's like a sidewalk in the park. I can see the huge city beyond the park. It's dusk and the lights of the buildings almost glow an emerald green color. It feels okay.

Next it shifts... and I'm sitting in a club in a booth... and there are three women or men sitting with there me. They are nice looking but look un-sexed... as if they don't know what gender they are. Ham- burg is there visiting with one of them.

I get up to go to the restroom. As I'm standing in the restroom... a man tries to come thru the door. I tell him it's occupied... he says okay and leaves.

The scene changes again... I'm walking on the city path again to a house I recognize. It jumps and then I'm driving... I see myself in a white car... and I'm trying to park it in a half circle driveway. I have trouble curbing the wheels... but finally everything is lined up and okay.

Now... I'm going to help a friend pack to move. As I look at the house ... it's a green flat topped adobe style house... with large windows. I see a mover's truck in front... and men loading the truck... and men inside packing. It feels like Mama San's house... but I don't see her. Then as I go in the front door... I see a friend who's a real estate broker... sitting behind a desk. She's taking a count of everything to make sure it's in order. She hands me a purse... and I feel like it's mine. She tells me to count the money. I count $500.00 and $200.00 ... then I hand the purse and the money back to her. She says, " Everything is in order." But she doesn't give me the purse or the money.

Then it shifts... I'm outside looking in the same house again... the house feels bare and empty. I go in and there is my sister... sitting behind the same desk. There is some sort of party gathering going on... people are sitting around talking. My sister is now writing out checks... as a gift to each person. As one man looks at his gift check... he looks shocked to see such a generous amount on the check. Everyone is amazed she gave him or her so much. I'm sitting there wondering... how much the amount is... and looking for a check for me... but she didn't write one for me. I felt very hurt and disappointed... like I was just a helper... and she didn't want to include me.

Next... my sister is walking around to the back of the house.

Dreams: The Money Jars

We are looking at vine covered fence walls... next to an alley... we come to a side gate and go in. She says, " the house is okay" ... that she just bought it. I can see... it has lots of dark red brick floors.

A time shift occurs... because it's now later and ... I see my sister and a puppy in the house. Newspapers cover the floor... and there are three separate plates for the dog to eat on. I say, " you should put the dog on the mat to eat out of the plates... so there's no mess." Next ... I look and she has a remote control... she pushes the button... and the mats swirl around to go up under each plate. Then I see food everywhere. She says, " next time ... I'll put the dog on the mats." But then she says, " No... the dog can eat outside... he's not living in this house."

The first part of the dream represents my worldly affairs and ideas... this is seen by the big crowded city. Here I am searching for parts of myself... and for my place in life. The music... is like the music in life... its good ...but then I want to leave to go to my room. The musicians that are helping me get there... are like the better worldly ideas... which are leading the way.

This was an interesting dream... because somtime later... parts of it had specfic meanings for me. In real life my Mama San passed over five days after this dream. Helping the friend to move and pack in the dream ...seems to relate this message of her death. I did pack and store her things in real life. As I was parking my car represented... that I've changed. I had trouble fitting the car into the half circle driveway... means that some things in me... no longer fit.

As for the money and the check in the dream... they relate to some feelings I had earlier. I didn't feel like any of Mama San's worldly possessions... would be left to me. Sure enough... that was true. Just like in the dream... I had to give the money back after I verified it... and at the party everyone else got a check...but I was left out. Thankfully... in real life I have a deeper understanding. But it does show me... how the human part of me... questions and wonders why. I truly appreciate my wonderful Mama San...her life's teachings and all those good times we shared. It's an experience that was grand!

I'm not real sure about the end of the dream... where my sister is saying the dog can eat outside. The dog represents a devotion of something ... but it's messy when it eats and needs mats. Its maybe that... the messy devotion... can go outside or it's leaving. It could have been a message... my Mama San was leaving and I would be outside.

The Big Jackpot ♥

I'm at the Las Vegas Club Casino in Las Vegas. I've been staying there for several days... with my friend. I see myself sitting at the machines... by the main casino cashiers cage. My friend is across the street at the Golden Gate Casino... playing his favorite video keno machines. There are not a lot of people around me at the machines...and the crowd is sparse.

I'm playing the Mega Millions dollar slot machine... which I rarely play. I'd been putting the maximum coins in... three dollars each time... but I just wasn't getting anything. I'm down to the last two coins... so I put them in and... it hits! I got Mega Million signs all the way across! As I look up... the lights are flashing... and I see the jackpot was Three Million dollars! But since I only had two coins in... I got $299,000.00 ...which was still good! I was so surprised... and I feel so excited.

A security guard walks up and congratulates me... and says, " WOW! Just one more coin." I say, "I know... but its still good."

The cashiers' cage that was beside me... now changes into a big stage... that's mostly bare. In the center is a host holding a microphone... he's congratulating me. He's asking me... to do some kind of performance on the stage. I say okay... but I want the security guard to come with me... to protect me and my jackpot.

This dream seemed so real... I wanted to go to Las Vegas... right away ... to see if it might come true. I didn't get to go in real life... at that time... so I didn't get the jackpot. To me the winning in the dream represents ... that I was winning at the game of life.

Since I had only two coins in... this means I only had part of the equation for big success. The jackpot was still big and good... but if I'd only had... the rest of the story or information (the other coin). WOW! My life would be even grander.

Then I was asked to be on stage... it like being on stage in life. I said okay... but I still wanted to be protected by the security guard... which means keeping myself secure and safe in life.

So in my dream... winning the money doesn't seem to mean... getting the money. But a winning at life... or what ever situation I'm in... or what I'm learning ...or trying to accomplish.

♥

The Casino Hotel Room ♥

In my dream... I realized we are in Las Vegas. My friend and some of his family... and myself are staying at a casino. I'm in the hotel room... and I can see... its painted bright white... it feels very refreshing and clean. Just beyond the doorway is a short hall... that leads to the main casino. Our bathroom is out in the hallway. I'm telling my friend... next time we get a room... I want one... with the bathroom inside our room. I don't want to have to walk outside... and he agrees.

I've decided to stay in the room...to clean up and rest. My friends have gone out to play in the casino... and I'll be meeting them later. I'm sitting there on the bed facing the white wall...and on the wall is a huge flat TV screen. But more than that... it's an electronic slot machine. My friend had been playing it before he left the room... and he also left some money in it... if I wanted to play. I'm sleepy... but I play some... I don't hit anything. Then... I think I must have fallen asleep.

Next... I'm up and trying to get dressed to meet my friends. I go to the bathroom in the hall...as I look beyond it I see... a very crowded casino. I decide I need to rest a little more and return to the room. I then sit in the bed facing the wall... and play the slot machine. When... I look at the size of the screen on the wall... I'm amazed how large it is... and that's it a slot machine too. I'm playing a slot game of lining up bars. I've won some... but then I hit a jackpot of $80.00. Then I hit another one... I see a bonus sign lighting up a number of coins... it goes 2000, 4000, 6000 & 8000... and stays on 8000. I won 8000 coins. I'm so excited I want to go tell my friend.

The scene changes... I'm standing in the hall... and I seem to be locked out of the room. There I am in bedclothes... with a big fluffy long white robe over them. I decide I should go out anyway to meet my friends.

The casino is packed with people. This is a newer casino...and I don't recognize it... or where anything is. I feel self-conscious being in my white robe. I start down an open hall... that leads to a larger area... filled with slot machines. I see a man in a suit with a radio... and I know he is an employee. I want to ask directions... but he's busy on his radio. Then I go on ... and start to walk thru a white folding door... but I realize there's a banquet inside for someone. I quickly step back and turn around.

The casino is just so big. I'm looking at the huge crystal chandeliers and the décor. It has lots of shops and places to eat. I seem to be standing in a courtyard. I watch the people for a while and all the movement around me. I can't find my friends... so I decide ... I'll go back to the room... even if I can't get in. Then... I'm wondering if my big jackpot is okay. I didn't cash it out... but left it on the wall slot machine... in the room.

I'm walking towards a row of slot machines... that are on the end of a wall... that divides two sections of the casino. I can see a white railing above... that protecting a walkway on an upper level. Down below... each machine is taken by a person... who's busily putting money in... hoping to get a jackpot.

Now... I'm near another long wide area... that leads towards our room. Then in the crowd... I see an older woman... dressed in a dark red long terry bathrobe...with her bedclothes underneath. I can see part of a shiny red silk nightgown... hanging below. I feel better... I'm not the only one in a robe. Maybe people will think ... I was at the pool... and I'm going to my room. I can see my white long robe and myself. I feel good... but a little out of place. As I'm walking... I'm listening to some conversations of the people talking. They are mostly talking about if they are winning... or where they'll be meeting someone.

The scene looks different now...as if I'm outdoors. There before me is... a long line of young girls dressed... in pale yellow

Dreams: The Money Jars

dresses. They are forming a circle... singing and dancing in line. At the back of the line is the teacher... an older lady. As I watch them ...I just keep walking on.

Next... I hear a lady beside me on a cell phone saying... that she didn't sleep at all last night... because of the bright flashing lights of some casino... that was right next to her window. She steps over a short cement wall... and I notice we are going towards the parking lot.

Then I'm near a gate and I bump into a tree... that's about five feet tall... but its all-dead branches... and one of the branches breaks off ...and falls to the ground. The lady looks at me... and says she has to hurry to meet her family. I look in the distance... I can see my friend and his family. I'm now watching... some other people in front of me... they are acting silly and cutting up.

As I get past a few of them...in the distance... in the parking lot...I see a motorcycle... that's painted a very handsome... black and turquoise. I immediately recognize it... as the hotel room with the wall slot machine inside. The hotel room has changed into a motorcycle... and my jackpot is on a screen... that's now part of it. I see my friends just waiting for me... as they can see I'm coming down the path toward them. There aren't any other cars or people... just my friends and the motorcycle... in a big parking lot. Next ...I'm wondering how did... the four of us get to the casino on one motorcycle?

The casino represents... a place of leisure time and fun... while the hotel represents... a place of transformation. The message relates to me in real life in this way: I'm working at home ...writing... and it does feel more like leisure time. A transformation is taking place... as I learn to create from home... not from the outside world. Its comfortable for me... and this is seen as... me being dressed in my white fluffy robe... in the dream.

It also feels like... I'm taking the time out from other things... because I stayed in the room to rest... and my friends went on into the casino. But it pays off... I hit a jackpot twice... as I play the

61

wall slot machine. Since the slot machine is in the wall… this means the wall is something …I have surrounded myself with. To me this means… my books I'm writing. I'm in a place of transformation… that pays off… and later I'll join my friends.

Then as the hotel room becomes a motorcycle… this is intriguing. For me it means… my place of transformation… is becoming more streamlined. A motorcycle is a more streamlined method of transportation. As I progress… things are more streamlined also… and the jackpot is still there too… and I have my friends along the way.

The Mafia
"Asking Godfather" ♥

I was going into a large buffet house to eat. My main reason to be here was I wanted an appointment with the Godfather…to ask for money. I was seated at a table near the center of the room…at the table with me was what I called the Godmother. She was kind of average looking…but very stern and powerful. She didn't smile …kept to the business at hand…didn't really acknowledge me…but knew I was there. She said he (Godfather) couldn't meet me just yet…he had some business to take care of.

As I looked at the table… it was old and wooden…in the center was a huge tray filled with succulent, tender, slightly barbequed meats… Godfather's favorite. I started to eat. It was so wonderfully good… and it was gone before I knew it. The Godmother and I got up to refill our plates.

On the way back to the table… I saw an old friend in line for the buffet. We hugged each other as we said hello. He said, " I see you are here with the Godmother." I replied, "Yes…I guess she has adopted me" and then she slightly smiled at me. The tension eased up and I knew everything would be okay.

Next, I was told I could freshen up… as I would get my audience with Godfather soon. I went in to comb my hair…I noticed it seemed really gray…I wanted to touch it up with color. As I started…a man walked in with a silver tray, which had the hair color on it. He said, " Here let me help you." The luscious consistency of the hair color just seemed to melt into my hair. It was a beautiful dark plum brown color. My hair felt so wonderful. Then I saw myself... I had that beautiful dark hair...piled thickly up on my head. My complexion was a beautiful clear olive tone... and I had on fuchsia lipstick. I almost looked Japanese...I felt so good.

I heard a voice saying it's time. I got up and looked at myself again. I had a small smudge of hair color on the right side of my nose. I tried to wipe it off...but when I did... it came back. Suddenly it didn't seem to matter.

After that, I was led into a large Victorian furnished room. It was filled with office furniture and over stuffed chairs. At the center was the Godfather...wearing a very pale light blue suit. He was very stern and powerful...and very much to the business at hand. Godfather was surrounded by several of his men and bodyguards. As I looked at him... I was nervous...I said my affirmation that I say in my awake state..." I am a Multi-Millionaire and I express this now." He knew exactly what I was asking for... money...to become a Multi-Millionaire in real life.

Then from his group of men...one spoke out. It was an old friend of mine from a past job at the Post Office. He said to the Godfather " I've already checked her out... and she's legit. I took the fingerprints from her voter registration card and checked them...she's okay." He said " I knew she was okay from the day I first walked into her house. It was filled with beautiful things...just like she is." I knew my request had been granted from Godfather and I woke up.

By going directly to Godmother and Godfather... I went to the highest source of power and control to make my request known. I wanted money in the physical world... so in my dream I went to those in control. They represent the positive and creative parts of me. The meat on the table was like... the ideas of life were... on the table as the meat of life. It was so wonderful... it disappeared easily as we ate and we wanted more.

The color in my hair represents... that I like the differences in wisdoms that hair is associated with. I wanted my hair fresh and beautiful.

Dreams: The Money Jars

    The old friend in the group…who was from the past PO job is a part of myself or my ideas. A part that knows me and that I'm okay with money and its use.

    In my real life I had been using affirmations to get better control over my thoughts of money. I continue to use them, knowing my request are granted. Godfather truly is with me.

The Violet Ah-Ha Moment ♥

I'm in a casino I don't recognize…and I'm putting a dollar bill in a slot machine. I'm wishing I had more money to play on. My friend is there … he's from East India. He has dark hair… but he's deceitful and underhanded. He's been putting fake money in the machines to play. At first the machine takes it… then breaks down later.

I ask him how much real money does he have… he says not much. Then I see him go to an ATM machine and get out $1700.00… and hide it in his coat. As I look across the casino… I see several machines broken down …and in the center of each are torn fake papers…that had been used for money. I see security guards sitting and talking over the situation. They are looking for this man… but he's not there now.

It changes… and I'm sitting at a party with several ladies in a long room. We are all very nicely dressed… just enjoying ourselves. A nicely decorated table is in front of us … with all kinds of food. It seems to be like a bridal party.

One of the younger women opens a package or gift… it has some beautiful open-lace jackets in it. One is mauve colored and some are white… they are all so beautiful and delicate. My mouth opens to ask… where did her friend find them? Just then an old girlfriend…Robin ask the same question. Robin looks at me and says, " Ah-Ha, that's the violet moment!" I feel glad and surprised to see her. I ask, " What is the violet ah-ha moment?" She says, "

67

It's when two people are thinking of the exact same thing at the same time ... or the same question."

The girl tell us that her mother made the beautiful jackets... Robin and I agree... we'd love to meet her. We walk to the back and there's another room... like part of a house. The mother is very nice and kind... she has white hair and is in a turquoise suit. She shows us a cuff of white lace with long white silky fringe on it. She says, " One day I was working... sewing this... and my daughter said " What a beautiful glove. You know you could just extend that into a lovely lace jacket." So I did. It's been a hit ever since."

We go back to the party now. As we get back to our table... I see my punch glass is empty. I tell Robin... I'm going for more. I walk back towards what I thought was a serving area. I could see kitchen workers and servers there... but as I walked in I realized... it was a huge celebration banquet for some other wonderful ladies.

The ladies were all extremely well dressed and very prosperous looking. I saw fine chocolates, fancy drinks and fine dishes on each table. The room was very long with lots of tables... and each table crowded to its capacity. I said, " Excuse me " ... and turned around to leave... as I do there is now a room on the other side of me... filled with more ladies seated at tables. They belong to the same banquet... and I see all fine chocolates and drinks on the tables. I'm trying to get back to the other side but can't.

The casino represents a place of leisure time and fun. I'm wanting to have more money to use... or more things of value for myself in life.

The male friend is an older part of myself... that doesn't recognize the rightful use of money. Hopefully I've grown past this... as I sure recognize what he is doing in the dream. It's like I or he hides the true money... and uses a fake to try to gain his winnings.

The party was a place of celebration...a place of a feast...with all the foods and drinks. The wedding gifts represented... a gift of new ideas in my own real life...and this is true... especially with my new writing projects. Seeing my old friend Robin… is like being reunited with a past creativity… that's part of me… I'd long forgotten about.

The violet ah-ha moment… adds a touch of magic. Its like we do find those moments in life… the magic is there for us. Getting to see how the lace jackets were made… was great. That means… I got to see how one creative ideas leads to another… to create something… even more lovely, beautiful and spectacular. The banquet for the prosperous ladies… represents this too. Wealth always leads to more wealth and fine things … or at least to me it means this.

In real life… I should just stay at the banquet…I wonder why I didn't in the dream? I woke up feeling so good inside.

The Wal-Mart Refund ♥

I was standing in a check out line at Wal-Mart. There was an older lady with white hair…wearing a white shirt… that was the cashier. When I was next in line…I told her I wanted a refund for this item. She handed me a return slip to fill out…which I did and gave back to her. As she looked over the receipts…I could see this look come over her. She became very rude, indignant and demeaning... telling me... No! That she couldn't do a refund and…how could she know that… I had not switched the item in the bag…which was a curtain.

I stated to her clearly " I want my refund." She said, "Well, you'll have to get a store manager to do it." As I looked over the store I saw a lady manager near the women's clothes.

The lady manager was very pretty…maybe of Hispanic decent …middle aged with shoulder length dark hair. She was wearing a very nice outfit…it was a greenish-gold moss colored vest over a pretty pink shirt and a floral skirt. I remember seeing her name tag…it said 'EL Monterey.' I thought what a different first name. As I got closer to her…she moved away…going down an isle straightening the clothes on the rack.

I had almost reached her…when a young man walked up to her to ask a question. Then again she walked away and I couldn't get her attention. I noticed that she was headed to the back of the store …where the lay-a-way department used to be…and where the offices are. Then another person stopped her to ask something. I said to myself " well, this time I'll just have to interrupt them to get her attention." So I did.

She was very polite… as was the other customer. I handed her my receipts and stated the problem with the cashier. She sat down on what looked like a large golden wood crate. She told me it was not a problem… then three or four very pretty East Indian women gathered around her. I guessed that they had come from the offices. They all agreed…my refund was in order.

The lady manager said " this time just take it to the lay-a-way counter back here …and they will give you your money." I knew I had my money. I was started in that direction when I woke up.

I feel that by being at Wal-Mart… it represents the shopping place of many ideas. I wanted my refund of money … meant that the item I purchased… or new ideas… was maybe not what I wanted. I wanted to go back to a prior item of value in my life. I had followed the correct steps in getting the refund…but the cashier was defiant. To me this means that once I took the ideas…that idea (cashier) did not want to… let go inside of me… and I needed the help of a manager.

It seemed that the manager moving away each time… was an illusive step in retrieving my money. My original idea kept moving away from me. I had to make a stand…which I did and state my position…then the manager was polite and receptive. There seemed to be an outside force... as seen by the East Indian girls working with the manager… that they were okaying my refund too.

Actually in real life… I'd been having some difficulties about money. I want to increase my cash flow… but it was slow in coming. I think the dream relates to this also. The manager moving away meant… my cash was slow in getting to me. The money was there for me… I just needed to find the right channels to get it.

Trees & Money ♥

I was walking along a path… outside in the fresh air. It feels like… I was trying to get away from the pressure of life. Things on the inside… were just too crowded and busy. I needed the time outside with nature.

As I walk along… I see a split rail fence dividing the green countryside. The trees and the air… feel dry. I decide to sit… in the midst of several large old cypress and juniper trees. I have my wooden chair with me… and move to the inside of the group of trees. Then as I'm sitting… I can only see the trees… and not the rest of the world or the scene around me. I'm completely surrounded by the big twenty-foot tall trees.

Then the wind comes up… and starts blowing in swirls… around the trees and me. The dead leaves start falling into the wind… as well as the dust. It's a windstorm… but I don't move. I sit there as the wind, leaves and dust swirl in the hot dry air… around me. I don't know how I can breathe… but for me this wind… feels good. I don't want to return to that other world of crowded places.

I watch… as the tiny green shapes of leaves float in the wind. Then a big gust of wind… swishes a pile of leaves and dust… from one side to the other… leaving bare earth at the bottom of the trees. For me… there just seems to be the feeling of the dry warm air… sweeping things away from me. I sit here in my chair a very long time. In a way… it's very peaceful here inside the windstorm. The wind blows away the old stuff… and you can get a glimpse of things being cleared and cleaned. It takes the pressure away… and leaves a fresh feeling… ready for new things to begin.

Then my scene changes… and its time for me to leave the

trees. I take my chair... and cross back to the path. Now the scene jumps... and I'm inside a very long white building. I see lots of beds... for people to sleep in... they look like hospital beds.

I'm walking around just looking... then someone catches my eye... and I stop to talk with them for a while. I see a few people in the distance... but I don't recognize them. We seem to talk over everyday things... and there is mutual understanding of life... with this person.

Now... the hallway of the building seems busy with people... coming and going... and we get interrupted. I want to freshen up before I leave. Someone is selling tickets to a lottery... so I buy a couple... and leave them with my friend at his bed. It seems he lives here in this place... it's like a big health care place... not really a hospital... or maybe it's some kind of dormitory.

As I walk down the hall to a visitors room... I see another friend. He seems eager to talk with me... but I ignore him... and I go in to wash up. As I'm splashing water on my face... I see my friend has gotten into a bed there... and he's waiting for me. He's got the fresh white sheets pulled up over him. I seem to be in a hurry... and don't want to talk with him... but he's trying to impress me and wants my attention. I walk out.

Then as I'm passing by the beds... on my way back to my other friend... I notice my lottery tickets from the corner of my eye. They are sitting on a table... and I see money attached to them. I immediately get the feeling and know... I won something. I'm excited... and now I know why my other friend was so eager to talk with me... I had won money.

My first friend takes... a rubber band and paper clips off the stacks of money. He says, " It's $550,000.00 - five hundred fifty thousand dollars." I see the vivid green of the money... and I feel the excitement of winning. It's a huge amount of money for me. I feel so fortunate and happy... to have won... especially when you don't expect to win.

Sometimes life does seem... like it's pressuring us... whether it's because of the outside world or our own selves. Sometimes we need to get away to nature. I feel like I've gone back... to a more natural part of myself... in real life too. Now... I'm weathering the windstorm... of change in my life... because I chose this. The windstorm represents... the spiritual forces blowing and changing... the trees and the dust or earth. This means releasing... some of my older values, old growth and ideas that no longer fit me... they are blown away.

Then as I go to the place where the hospital beds are... and I see my friend...this represents a place of healing inside myself... a place where some of my ideas are healed. I seem to ignore a part of myself... who's is the other male friend. To me he represents... an idea or thoughts that were much less favorable.... and I wanted to ignore it or him.

By ignoring the lesser ideas... I gained something of much more value. I won the lottery! This means... by staying true to my thoughts of creating more of what I want... and visualizing it...thinking about those thoughts... it manifested. I was the winner! My dream doesn't necessarily mean winning money... but you never know. For me... I had won at changing my life and healing my ideas.

Who's Driving? ♥

I'm looking out the windows of a car... watching the scenery go by. Looking at myself... I'm about 20 years old. My Dad is driving and Mom is there with him in the front seat. I'm watching from the back seat... just looking at jagged mountains on either side of the steep road. The mountains are rocky and brown in color... and covered in snow... but actually the snow is volcanic ash. The road winds upward and upward. I know we are in New Mexico... and it feels more like a family trip now. I feel safe in the car with them... even though we must be careful on the steep road. We seem to go right along.

The scene changes... and my friend is driving. I'm now in the front seat with him. I feel concerned about... his being in control of driving me. He's taking me to see his new house. We both live in the same city... but its not in New Mexico any longer. We are going along a highway... as I look out across the land... it's mostly flat with a few trees. We are approaching his place. All the neighborhood houses sit at an angle... lengthwise on the lots. His house has triangular shaped rooms... connected by cement patios. The house is made of sandstone bricks... and is partially built into the side of a hill. It's very modern, new and clean looking. It blends in so well with the natural elements.

As we are going to the house... I notice several of the plants outside need water. The triangular shaped landscaping... is interesting with tall plants... but they are drying up. I turn the garden hose on ...and lay it down to let the water soak in. Suddenly... my friend's kids are running past me... to get into the house... then his grandkids... a big black dog... two black and white cats... then a gray black cat. I feel over whelmed. We don't stay long at his house... then we are driving on.

I feel like... I'm inside of a car thru out this entire dream... and someone else is driving. I have to wait on them... or accept their decisions the whole time. I don't like the feeling of confinement. I get discouraged... because now... the scene jumps continually... from me going here and there with my friend. He's telling me... I can only do certain things. He leaves for a while... and then returns to take me somewhere else.

My friend has now changed into another man. I seem to recognize him from the past... maybe an old boyfriend. It doesn't feel good to be with him either. He has some problems with memory, drinking and just problems with life. He's driving me to my house... and I'm hoping to get there safely.

As I see my house... it looks odd. I see parts of rooms... that look back to the past. In one room... I see my sister... she's putting on latex gloves and cutting some gauze... to change the bandage on a patient in the room. I see her toss the glove and gauze aside... when she's finished. I'm trying desperately to tell her... not to toss them. The man who is with me is trying to frame her. He wants to kill the patient... and make it look like she did it... using her fingerprints from these items... then transferring them to the murder weapon. Before I can reach her... we are in the car again... going to a local bar.

Inside the bar... there are three of us now. A female friend has joined us. Next thing I know she is now been trained... and is the bartender standing behind the bar. I'm playing a strange looking slot machine at the bar. You stack the money or coins in a vertical slot... and it drops the coins one at a time down thru a slot. My friend is playing too... but he is very cautious as not to put to much money in. I stack the vertical slot full of gold coins... and they are falling fast thru the slots... but I'm not getting any hits or returns... I'm not winning. Then as I see the huge gold coins falling quickly... I want to win big in a hurry. My friend stops the coins... and tells me to go at a slower pace... make my chances pay off... not watch them fall thru.

Next... the woman bartender tells my friend to leave... that someone is looking for him. The two of us leave... and go to his house. He's pacing the floor. I know he won't be here much longer. I feel so frustrated. Why did I have to go down this road? And why these people? I want to be in my own car.

The car in the dream represents... some current circumstances in my life... and how I'm handling them. Who's in control... means which thoughts... have I let take over the driving in my life.

My Mom and Dad represent a balance in life for me... and I feel safe. Then as the car goes uphill... this represents a place where I'm achieving what I want... I'm moving forward.

The different men that take control... refer to different thoughts in my mind... that they took control. I see a lot of past issues... in the dream for me. One friend... it was issues with his kids and so on. The other friends... it was issues of compulsiveness... as gambling, drinking and murder. The murder meant... he wanted to kill of the creative part of me... and frame my sister to be rid of us both... then he'd have more control.

The dream is a viewing of past issues... but is it also a key to right now. I need to be in control of my thoughts and my body. So I can make the most of things... and let the past go... maximize my chances to win... and succeed in my efforts.

Winning

I'm in a casino with my friend and several of his men friends. They are playing the slot machines and talking. I'm just walking around... seeing if there's a machine I want to play. It feels okay to be here.

I find a machine that's all by itself near a bar. As I sit down... I'm thinking to myself...it probably won't do much... since it's at the end. I don't recognize the slot game...but I put my coins in and press the button. Nothing hits ...then all of a sudden it hits...and I got the jackpot!

I'm yelling to myself " I got it! I got it!" Then I yell out loud to my friend " Hon, I got it! I hit the jackpot!" But my voice is very soft...even though I'm yelling...he doesn't hear me and keeps talking to his buddies. I'm watching the screen on the machine to see what the jackpot is...it's flashing $1200.00...but then the screen starts moving and bonus games are playing. I'm wondering what to do... and at the same time wondering where is the slot person to pay me my money. Then the machine stops at $2600.00... It's flashing on the screen - $2600.00.

A cocktail waitress with a big headdress...like a show girl...comes over and says " Congratulations on winning the Banana Frappe' Daiquiri game." She sets a drink on the machine. It's a large margarita glass with a very long stem of about eight inches...all around the top rim of the glass are slices of banana...and a large piece of flat sweet bread in the center. I notice it looks just like her headdress.

A second waitress...rather plain looking... in a white shirt and black pants... walks over. She puts a very tall cylindrical glass...

next to the first drink...and it starts to fill its self with milk or cream. In my hand I have quarters...so I put some in her tip jar on the tray. She says thank you and leaves.

I now see a gentleman in a costume suit... bright and flashy... like Mardi Gars. He has a pad of papers in his hand...and is walking to me. He's the slot person to pay my jackpot to me. He's filling it out...it's mine. Then I wake up.

WOW!... what a wonderful dream! It's the kind of dream that's very rewarding... to the physical side of life... seeing all that money and the jackpot... even if just in the dream... feels so good. On the spiritual side of life it's winning that something... far more rewarding in our growth not just in money terms.

I see this as true in that... I see the jackpot amount flashing on the screen... but then it continues to add up more money... it represents both the physical and the spiritual.

The lush Banana Frappe Daiquiri means it was a gift of winning at something far more valuable than just the money... but winning in life. The second drink meant... the cream is the nurturing of life... and I had won both! (It's like a repeat of the first part of the message.)

My friend not hearing me... was that he chose not to receive the same valuable information... but to keep on playing.

I had been reading two new books in my real life...The Law of Attraction and The Secret. What a joy it is to discover my life and how it works... now I have the information to truly make and change my life... to a true success story.

♥

My Dream Symbols ♥

My Dream Symbols	What They Mean to Me
1. Houses	Parts of myself
2. People	People are the ideas or thoughts that I connect with that specific person. It's the idea of what they represent to me
3. Cars	My physical body
4. Water, rivers etc.	Vital element of life and spiritual life
5. Work or work places	Life's work or learning's
6. Toilets	Places of releasing the old
7. Shoes	My understanding
8. Cats or kitties	My female creative, intuitive side
9. Birds	Spiritual truths, messages
10. Windows	Looking into things or to higher ideas
11. Flying	Freedom from the physical

12. Clothing	Understanding
13. Being naked	Naked truth, nothing hidden
14. Killing	Ending of a situation or idea
15. Dogs	Faithful companions, devotion
16. Shopping	Looking for new ideas
17. Casino's	Pleasure time or entertainment
18. Actors	Performance of ideas, what I associate them with…not them personally
19. Sexual or sex	Physical creation, not of sexual nature
20. Desks	A place where we conduct our worldly affairs
21. Bugs	Things that bug you… past or present
22. Blood	Our physical life's force
23. Teeth falling out	Things lost in compromising… ourselves or our ideas
24. Hotels	Places of transformation

The Author ♥
"Mary Belle Claude"

I am a college graduate and have been a student of metaphysics for over 30 years. For several years in the past I had the honor of holding a degree within my study group.

My life changed dramatically in the late 1970's... as I began a life long Love... of learning the Truths of Life thru metaphysics. I read, studied and I took classes with a passion.

My friend, mentor and teacher on this journey will be known only as I call her... my " Mama-San," with her husband "Papa-San," together we were a family here... in the Hi- Desert of California. I became a part in their center for Spiritual Learning ..."The Eternal Light Center." I continued my studying thru the years... and doing what I could to help. I learned how very much we are all connected in life... and what some of the truths of life are for me.

It was thru all my classes and spiritual counseling's... that I learned of symbols and their meanings. It was not until after 2001... that I really started to pay attention to my dreams. Before that ... I might have some memorable ones... and others quickly faded completely. I started journaling the dreams and putting meanings to them. As I did ...the more the dreams came and then ...the more the relevance showed up between my sleep life and my awake life.

I have read and studied many dream books also...but continue to use how each interpretation pertains to my life and me. So now it is that... I continue with each day... /or should I say each night's dream... as a new chapter in my life ...and in my book.

You truly are a wonderful Dream Star.
Make it an Exceptional performance! You are always the STAR!

DREAM BIG !!!

Also By Mary Belle Claude

Dreams: A Clear Penny

ARE YOU A DREAMER? EVER WONDER WHERE THEY ALL COME FROM? Maybe you're able to interpret and learn some of the meanings to your dreams. There are so, so many books of symbols and interpretations out there. BUT - did you ever wonder what other people dream --??? WELL - HERE'S THE BOOK! A book of real Dreams from the Author that are almost short stories in themselves. By New Author " Mary Belle Claude " Even the Pen Name, the Book Titles and Book Covers ... came from a "dream." See if you see and share some of the same insights as the author. SWEET DREAMS! FIRST IN A FOUR PART SERIES

1. DREAMS: A CLEAR PENNY
2. DREAMS: DOLLARS ON A ROLL
3. DREAMS: HUNDREDS OF HUNDREDS
4. DREAMS: MILLIONS CLEARLY STATED

NEW BOOK - DREAMS: THE MONEY JARS (WHAT IF YOU DREAMED - ABOUT MONEY?)

Learn more at:
www.outskirtspress.com/dreamsmarybelleclaude

Also By Mary Belle Claude

Dreams: Dollars on a Roll

ARE YOU A DREAMER? EVER WONDER WHERE THEY ALL COME FROM? Maybe you are able to interpret and learn some of the meanings to your dreams. There are so, so many books of symbols and interpretations out there. BUT - did you ever wonder what other people dream --???WELL - HERE IS THE BOOK ! A book of real Dreams from the Author that are almost short stories in themselves. By New Author; Mary Belle Claude. Even the Pen Name, the Book Titles and Book Covers came from a dream. See if you see and share some of the same insights as the author. SWEET DREAMS! SECOND IN A FOUR PART SERIES
1. DREAMS: A CLEAR PENNY
2. DREAMS: DOLLARS ON A ROLL
3. DREAMS: HUNDREDS OF HUNDREDS
4. DREAMS: MILLIONS CLEARLY STATED

NEW BOOK - DREAMS: THE MONEY JARS (WHAT IF YOU DREAMED - ABOUT MONEY?) Coming Soon.

Learn more at:
www.outskirtspress.com/dreams2mbc

Printed in the United States
150633LV00003B/251/A